Name: Charlie and Daisy Brown

Age: 5 and 2

Hello!!

I'm so excited to see you here!

I know you have been looking forward to the summer holidays for ages! Well, it is finally here! Lots of free time to have tons of fun and no need to get up super early because there's NO school. Hopefully, there will be lots of sunny days, too!

I've put together this journal for you to store all the amazing things you get up to. I can't wait for you to get started. There are only 3 rules in this journal:
1. Have lots of fun
2. Fill the pages with as much colour as you can
3. Remember there are no right or wrong answers here. You can write anything you like.

I hope you have a wonderful summer and smile lots.

See you soon

Fran :)

Because   no more school. Enjoying the sunshine.

CB = I like to stay asleep all morning   LOL LOL

DB = Having Charlie home, I want him to be my best friend.

Daddy = Spending time with everybody.

Mummy = Lazier mornings, making memories, watching Charlie
and Daisy play, time as a family, my birthday :)

I can't wait to

Fill all the white space on this page using all the colours that make you
think of summer

MY SUMMER BUCKET LIST

Make a list of all the things you would love to do this summer. Then tick off all the ones you have done.

- Go on a bus ✓
- Go on a tube ✓
- Go on a train ✓
- Go on a tram.
- Go to the seaside - Salt and Vinegar chips.
- Soft Play ✓
- Park. ✓
- Play with Molly. ✓
- Birthday Breakfast.
- Party
- Build the tallest tower.
- Jumping from taller heights

Need ideas? Head to the Idea Factory at the back of your journal!

THIS SUMMER I WANT TO READ...

Make a list of all the amazing books you would love to read this summer. Then tick off all the ones you have read

The Gruffalo

Stick Man.

My summer reading goal is ____10____ books!

I achieved this on_______________________

and I feel_____________________

TRYING NEW THINGS IS GREAT!

Make a list of all the new things you would love to try this summer. Then tick off all the ones you have done.

Need ideas? Head to the Idea Factory at the back of your journal!

WEEK

ONE

When I woke up I felt _HOT!_

Last night I dreamt _______________

Describe what you did today in as much detail as you can

Played in the garden.
Somebody viewed the house
and put in an offer.
Played at Grandma and Grandads.
Mummy went out for dinner.
Daddy was at work.

On the next page, write down as many words as you can think of to describe your perfect summer day.

THEN ~~come back here and talk about how well you~~ did

Mummy lost her phone (in the house!) and was
convinced it had been stolen ..... found it under
the chair in the kitchen.

The best thing I did today was:

Had 4 Bedtime Stories
with Aunty Roo

Word of the day:

CB = That means laughing

GIGGLE

DB = Errr I dont know.

Did you try anything new today? What was it?

Saturday.
21st July 2018.

When I woke up I felt _Excited._

____

Last night I dreamt _______________________

____

Describe what you did today in as much detail as you can

Got up and went to Bluewater
Shopping with Aunty Roo.
Had lunch @ Nandos/KFC
Drove to Horton Kirby for
Bouncy Castle fun with Molly
and Georgie.
Played at Grandma and Grandads.

____

____

____

____

On the next page, draw a cat using only triangles

. THEN come back here and talk about how well you did

The best thing I did today was:

BOUNCY CASTLE

____

Word of the day:

CB = It changes to dark at night

DB = Points up in the air.

Did you try anything new today? What was it?

____

____

____

____

____

____

____

Sunday 22nd July 2018

When I woke up I felt **Hot!**

Last night I dreamt _______________

Describe what you did today in as much detail as you can

Charlie went to Asda with Mummy to get Picnic food.

Daisy went to the Post Office with Daddy.

We all went to the ruins to meet Feby, Dwiko, Jaxen, Alison, Leon and Rowan.

We had a picnic and played ball and badminton.

Mummy went to Garrys funeral.

Daddy, Daisy and Charlie played in the sprinkler in the Garden.

On the next page, draw all the things you love about the summer holidays.

THEN come back here and talk about how well you did

The best thing I did today was:

Playing with our friends.

Word of the day:

CB = It means you have to tidy up.

MESSY

DB = Points to all the Duplo on the floor.

Did you try anything new today? What was it?

Monday 23rd July 2018.

When I woke up I felt _Hot !_____________

Last night I dreamt _____________________

Describe what you did today in as much detail as you can

Mummy went to work.
Daddy took Charlie and Daisy
on 2 trains and a bus to
see Nanny Sue and Grandad
Colin.
Mummy went to Croydon to
have dinner with everyone
and drive home in the car.

On the next page, write down a words beginning with every letter of the alphabet.

THEN come back here and talk about how well you did

The best thing I did today was:

Went on trains.

Word of the day:

CB = Like you can get at sainsburys or Asda.

ORANGE

DB = Picked up an orange magnet

Did you try anything new today? What was it?

Tuesday 24th July 2018.

When I woke up I felt_______________________

____

Last night I dreamt _______________________

____

Describe what you did today in as much detail as you can

____
____
____
____
____
____
____
____
____
____

On the next page, draw yourself as a superhero (make one up).

THEN come back here and talk about how well you did

The best thing I did today was:

____
____
____

Word of the day:

CB = To lay down and watch TV.

RELAX

DB = To go to bed.

Did you try anything new today? What was it?

____
____
____

Daisy started POTTY TRAINING !!

____

____

Wednesday 25th July 2018.

When I woke up I felt_______________
____

Last night I dreamt _______________
____

Describe what you did today in as much detail as you can

____
____
____
____
____
____
____
____
____
____

On the next page, write a poem using today's word of the day (juggle).

THEN come back here and talk about how well you did

____
____
____

The best thing I did today was:

____
____
____

Word of the day:
CB = Started moving his hands in juggling motion.

JUGGLE

DB = looks at CB and asks him.

Did you try anything new today? What was it?

____
____
____

When I woke up I felt________________

____

Last night I dreamt ________________

____

Describe what you did today in as much detail as you can

____
____
____
____
____
____
____
____
____
____
____

On the next page, draw the most amazing ice cream you can imagine.

THEN come back here and talk about how well you did

____
____
____
____

The best thing
I did today was:

____
____
____

Word of the day:
CB= what grown ups eat.
DOUGHNUT
DB= You are a doughnut mummy.

Did you try anything new today? What was it?

____
____
____

WEEK

TWO

DAY 8

When I woke up I felt _______________

____

Last night I dreamt _______________

____

Describe what you did today in as much detail as you can

____
____
____
____
____
____
____
____
____
____

On the next page, cut and stick some things that show us what you did last week. Don't forget to get help if you need it!

THEN come back here and talk about how well you did

____
____
____
____

The best thing I did today was:

____
____
____

Word of the day:

DB = Errr I dont know

QUEST

CB = Too ask a question

Did you try anything new today? What was it?

____
____
____

When I woke up I felt________________

____

Last night I dreamt ________________

____

Describe what you did today in as much detail as you can

____
____
____
____
____
____
____
____
____
____

On the next page, explore all the ways you could use a button (the more random and weird ways the better).

THEN come back here and talk about how well you did

____

____

____

____

The best thing I did today was:

____
____
____

Word of the day:

CB = Its what you wear on your coat to do it up.

BUTTON

DB = Its chocolate

Did you try anything new today? What was it?

____
____
____

When I woke up I felt_______________
____

Last night I dreamt ________________
____

Describe what you did today
in as much detail as you can

____
____
____
____
____
____
____
____
____
____
____

Use the next page to explore
how you could invent a time
machine using only toilet roll
tubes.

THEN come back here and talk
about how well you did

____
____
____
____

The best thing
I did today was:

____
____
____

Word of the day:

MUNCH

Did you try anything
new today? What
was it?

____
____
____

When I woke up I felt ___________________

____

Last night I dreamt ___________________

____

Describe what you did today in as much detail as you can

____
____
____
____
____
____
____
____
____
____
____

On the next page, draw a character from your favourite book

THEN come back here and talk about how well you did

____
____
____
____

The best thing I did today was:

____
____
____

Word of the day:

SQUIGGLE

Did you try anything new today? What was it?

____
____
____

When I woke up I felt_______________

____

Last night I dreamt _______________

____

Describe what you did today in as much detail as you can

On the next page, write or draw all the things that make you amazing.

THEN come back here and talk about how well you did

The best thing I did today was:

Word of the day:

CLAPTRAP

Did you try anything new today? What was it?

When I woke up I felt_________________

____

Last night I dreamt __________________

____

Describe what you did today in as much detail as you can

____
____
____
____
____
____
____
____
____
____

On the next page, write about or draw funniest thing you have ever seen.

THEN come back here and talk about how well you did

The best thing I did today was:

____
____
____

Word of the day:

LIZARD

Did you try anything new today? What was it?

____
____
____

____
____
____

When I woke up I felt _______________

____

Last night I dreamt _______________

____

Describe what you did today in as much detail as you can

____
____
____
____
____
____
____
____
____
____

On the next page, have a friend or family member write something about you.

THEN come back here and talk about how well you did

The best thing I did today was:

____
____
____

Word of the day:

CRUMPLE

Did you try anything new today? What was it?

____
____
____

____

____

____

WEEK
THREE

When I woke up I felt_________________

____

Last night I dreamt_________________

____

Describe what you did today in as much detail as you can

____
____
____
____
____
____
____
____
____

On the next page, cut and stick some things that show us what you did last week. Don't forget to get help if you need it!

THEN come back here and talk about how well you did

____
____
____

The best thing I did today was:

____
____
____

Word of the day:

ALIEN

Did you try anything new today? What was it?

____
____
____

When I woke up I felt_______________

____

Last night I dreamt_________________

____

Describe what you did today in as much detail as you can

____
____
____
____
____
____
____
____
____
____

On the next page, write about or draw what you think life would be like if you were your favourite animal.

THEN come back here and talk about how well you did

The best thing
I did today was:

____
____
____

Word of the day:

WEATHER

Did you try anything new today? What was it?

____
____
____

____
____
____
____

When I woke up I felt________________

____

Last night I dreamt _________________

____

Describe what you did today in as much detail as you can

____
____
____
____
____
____
____
____
____
____

On the next page, write a story about three kids who get to experience a summer holiday that never ends.

THEN come back here and talk about how well you did

____
____
____

The best thing I did today was:

____
____
____

Word of the day:

FLIPPER

Did you try anything new today? What was it?

____
____
____

When I woke up I felt _______________

____

Last night I dreamt _______________

____

Describe what you did today
in as much detail as you can

____
____
____
____
____
____
____
____
____
____
____

On the next page, write a story
about the mysterious goblin
that you just found in your
bathtub.

THEN come back here and talk
about how well you did

____
____
____

The best thing
I did today was:

____
____
____

Word of the day:

GOBLIN

Did you try anything
new today? What
was it?

____
____
____

When I woke up I felt________________

____

Last night I dreamt ____________________

____

Describe what you did today in as much detail as you can

____
____
____
____
____
____
____
____
____

Fill the next page with as many different colour zig-zags as you can.

THEN come back here and talk about how well you did

The best thing I did today was:

____
____
____

Word of the day:

ZIG-ZAG

Did you try anything new today? What was it?

____
____
____

____

____

____

When I woke up I felt_______________

____

Last night I dreamt___________________

____

Describe what you did today
in as much detail as you can

____
____
____
____
____
____
____
____
____
____
____

On the next page, write about
(or draw) a day when you had
the most fun you've ever had.

THEN come back here and talk
about how well you did

The best thing
I did today was:

____
____
____

Word of the day:

HOKUM

Did you try anything
new today? What
was it?

____
____
____

____
____
____
____

When I woke up I felt_________________

____

Last night I dreamt _______________

____

Describe what you did today in as much detail as you can

____
____
____
____
____
____
____
____
____
____
____

On the next page, write a poem about sunshine or clouds (or both if you like).

THEN come back here and talk about how well you did

____
____
____

The best thing I did today was:

____
____
____

Word of the day:

YOGHURT

Did you try anything new today? What was it?

____
____
____

WEEK

FOUR

When I woke up I felt _______________________

____

Last night I dreamt _______________________

____

Describe what you did today in as much detail as you can

____
____
____
____
____
____
____
____
____
____
____

On the next page, cut and stick some things that show us what you did last week. Don't forget to get help if you need it!

THEN come back here and talk about how well you did

____
____
____

The best thing I did today was:

____
____
____

Word of the day:

PIE

Did you try anything new today? What was it?

____
____
____

When I woke up I felt_________________

____

Last night I dreamt _______________

____

Describe what you did today
in as much detail as you can

____
____
____
____
____
____
____
____
____
____

On the next page, write down
as many words as you
can make with the letters in
SUMMER HOLIDAY.

THEN come back here and talk
about how well you did

____

____

____

The best thing
I did today was:

____
____
____

Word of the day:

UPPITY

Did you try anything
new today? What
was it?

____
____
____

When I woke up I felt________________

____

Last night I dreamt________________

____

Describe what you did today
in as much detail as you can

____

____

____

____

____

____

____

____

____

____

On the next page, design a
brand new board game that
you wish existed.

THEN come back here and talk
about how well you did

The best thing
I did today was:

____

____

____

Word of the day:

JABBER

Did you try anything
new today? What
was it?

____

____

____

____

____

____

When I woke up I felt_______________

Last night I dreamt _______________

Describe what you did today
in as much detail as you can

On the next page, explore all
the ways you could use a sock
(the more random and weird
ways the better).

THEN come back here and talk
about how well you did

The best thing
I did today was:

Word of the day:

VANISH

Did you try anything
new today? What
was it?

When I woke up I felt_______________

____

Last night I dreamt _______________

____

Describe what you did today
in as much detail as you can

____
____
____
____

____
____
____
____
____
____
____

Try and discover something
new today. On the next page,
write about (or draw) what
you've discovered,

THEN come back here and talk
about how well you did

____
____
____

The best thing
I did today was:

____
____
____

Word of the day:

MOOMIN

Did you try anything
new today? What
was it?

____
____
____

When I woke up I felt_______________

____

Last night I dreamt _______________

____

Describe what you did today
in as much detail as you can

____
____
____

____
____
____
____
____

____

On the next page, make up a
song about today's word of the
day (popcorn).

THEN come back here and talk
about how well you did

The best thing
I did today was:

____
____
____

Word of the day:

POPCORN

Did you try anything
new today? What
was it?

____
____
____

____

____

____

When I woke up I felt __________________

____

Last night I dreamt __________________

____

Describe what you did today in as much detail as you can

____
____
____
____
____
____
____
____
____
____
____

On the next page, write about (or draw) what your dream job would be when you grow up. What would it involve?

THEN come back here and talk about how well you did

____
____
____

The best thing I did today was:

____
____
____

Word of the day:

RUMBLE

Did you try anything new today? What was it?

____
____
____

WEEK

FIVE

When I woke up I felt_______________

____

Last night I dreamt_______________

____

Describe what you did today in as much detail as you can

____
____
____
____
____
____
____
____
____
____

On the next page, cut and stick some things that show us what you did last week. Don't forget to get help if you need it!

THEN come back here and talk about how well you did

____
____
____

The best thing I did today was:

____
____
____

Word of the day:

ZAPPER

Did you try anything new today? What was it?

____
____
____

When I woke up I felt_________________

____

Last night I dreamt_____________________

____

Describe what you did today in as much detail as you can

____
____
____
____
____
____
____
____
____
____

On the next page, write a list (or draw) of all the things that make you happy.

THEN come back here and talk about how well you did

The best thing I did today was:

____
____
____

Word of the day:

HAPPY

Did you try anything new today? What was it?

____
____
____

____

____

____

When I woke up I felt_______________

____

Last night I dreamt _______________

____

Describe what you did today in as much detail as you can

____
____
____
____
____
____
____
____
____
____
____

On the next page, write a list (or draw) of all the things that are your favourite colour.

THEN come back here and talk about how well you did

The best thing I did today was:

____
____
____

Word of the day:

ALIKE

Did you try anything new today? What was it?

____
____
____

____
____
____

When I woke up I felt_______________

____

Last night I dreamt ________________

____

Describe what you did today
in as much detail as you can

____

____

____

____

____

____

____

____

____

____

Try and find a really cool way
to make the next page shiny.

THEN come back here and talk
about how well you did

The best thing
I did today was:

____

____

____

Word of the day:

SHINY

Did you try anything
new today? What
was it?

____

____

____

____

____

____

When I woke up I felt_____________________

____

Last night I dreamt _____________________

____

Describe what you did today in as much detail as you can

____
____
____
____
____
____
____
____
____
____

On the next page, write about (or draw) how sunshine makes you feel.

THEN come back here and talk about how well you did

The best thing I did today was:

____
____
____

Word of the day:

ALOOF

Did you try anything new today? What was it?

____
____
____

____
____
____
____

DAY 34

When I woke up I felt_________________

Last night I dreamt _________________

Describe what you did today in as much detail as you can

On the next page, design your very own rollercoaster. Think about exactly what you would like to happen when you were riding it.

THEN come back here and talk about how well you did

The best thing I did today was:

Word of the day:

BUMBLE

Did you try anything new today? What was it?

When I woke up I felt _______________

____

Last night I dreamt _______________

____

Describe what you did today in as much detail as you can

____
____
____
____
____
____
____
____
____
____
____

On the next page, draw a map to help you find some imaginary treasure you have hidden.

THEN come back here and talk about how well you did

____

____

The best thing I did today was:

____
____
____

Word of the day:

HIDDEN

Did you try anything new today? What was it?

____
____
____

WEEK SIX

When I woke up I felt_______________

____

Last night I dreamt _______________

____

Describe what you did today
in as much detail as you can

____
____
____
____
____
____
____
____
____
____

On the next page, cut and stick
some things that show us
what you did last week. Don't
forget to get help if you need
it!

THEN come back here and talk
about how well you did

____
____
____

The best thing
I did today was:

____
____
____

Word of the day:

PLUMMET

Did you try anything
new today? What
was it?

____
____
____

When I woke up I felt________________

____

Last night I dreamt________________

____

Describe what you did today
in as much detail as you can

____
____
____
____
____
____
____
____
____
____

Use the next page to explore
what life would be like if there
was no school. Ever.

THEN come back here and talk
about how well you did

The best thing
I did today was:

____
____
____

Word of the day:

OXYGEN

Did you try anything
new today? What
was it?

____
____
____

____
____
____

When I woke up I felt________________

____

Last night I dreamt __________________

____

Describe what you did today in as much detail as you can

____
____
____
____
____
____
____
____
____
____

On the next page, write about (or draw) what life would be like if you could do magic. What spell would you do first?

THEN come back here and talk about how well you did

____
____
____

The best thing I did today was:

____
____
____

Word of the day:

WIZARD

Did you try anything new today? What was it?

____
____
____

When I woke up I felt_______________

____

Last night I dreamt_______________

____

Describe what you did today in as much detail as you can

____
____
____
____
____
____
____
____
____
____

On the next page, write a list of (or draw) all the best things you have done this summer.

THEN come back here and talk about how well you did

The best thing I did today was:

____
____
____

Word of the day:

SMUSH

Did you try anything new today? What was it?

____
____
____

____

____

When I woke up I felt_______________

____

Last night I dreamt ________________

____

Describe what you did today
in as much detail as you can

____
____
____
____

____
____
____

____

____

Use the next page to explore all
the things you're looking
forward to when you go back
to school in a few days time.

THEN come back here and talk
about how well you did

____

____

____

The best thing
I did today was:

____
____
____

Word of the day:

ELF

Did you try anything
new today? What
was it?

____
____
____

When I woke up I felt_____________

____

Last night I dreamt _______________

____

Describe what you did today in as much detail as you can

____
____
____
____

____
____
____
____
____
____

On the next page, invent a brand new subject that you would teach at school if you were a teacher.

THEN come back here and talk about how well you did

The best thing I did today was:

____
____
____

Word of the day:

PIRATE

Did you try anything new today? What was it?

____
____
____

____

____

____

When I woke up I felt_______________

____

Last night I dreamt _______________

____

Describe what you did today in as much detail as you can

____
____
____
____

____
____
____
____
____

____

____

On the next page, write or draw all the things you would like to achieve in the next year.

THEN come back here and talk about how well you did

The best thing
I did today was:

____
____

____

Word of the day:

YOLK

Did you try anything new today? What was it?

____
____

____

____
____
____
____

THE IDEA FACTORY

USING THE WORD OF THE DAY

- Teach yourself what it means (if you don't know)
- Use it in a story
- Write a poem about it
- Sing a song about it
- Use it in a full sentence as many times as you can throughout the day
- Try and see if you can find it written in any books, magazines or newspapers
- Try and get an adult to say it (without them knowing)
- Try and get an adult to say it in a conversation (they need to know this time!)
- Try and make different words using the letters
- Write an acrostic poem using the word
- Write a letter to someone explaining what the word means
- Pretend you are on the news and present a story about it.
- Try and learn how to say it backwards

BUCKET LIST IDEAS

- Learn how to say hello in three different languages
- Make up your own language
- Film your own TV show (like a daily news show)
- Learn to bake a cake
- Conduct a scientific experiment (safely)
- Run/walk/cycle a certain distance
- Go a whole day without watching TV or playing computer games
- Write a long story
- Create something that takes longer than an hour
- Read a certain number of books
- Go to the beach
- Make up your own dance
- Make up your own game and write the rules yourself
- Learn how to say the alphabet backwards
- Keep your bedroom extra tidy
- Discover a new interesting fact every day
- Do something helpful every day
- Make the tallest tower possible out of sticks

NEW THINGS YOU COULD TRY

- New types of foods
- New types of books
- New types of films or TV shows
- New types of sports
- New types of writing
- New types of drawing and painting
- New types of crafts
- New outdoor games
- New indoor games
- New types of drinks
- New types of music to dance to
- New places to go
- New languages to try and learn
- New places to sit and read
- Meeting new people
- Discover new uses for every day objects
- New hobbies
- New ways to have fun
- New ways to express yourself
- New ways to keep active

GET IDEAS FROM ADULTS YOU KNOW

This Journal was
brought to you by

www.thehappyjournals.com

Printed in Great Britain
by Amazon